Multiplication and Division

AGE 5-7

Rhona Whiteford and Jim Fitzsimmons
Illustrated by Sascha Lipscomb

As a parent, you can play an important role in your child's education by your interest and encouragement. This book is designed to help your child become confident in the vital mathematical skills of multiplication and division. There are six sections, each with a short test.

How to help your child

- Keep sessions short and regular. Your child will learn more effectively if you approach the exercises as an enjoyable challenge, rather than an unpleasant chore.

- Build your child's confidence by offering lots of praise and encouragement. Rather than simply pointing out that an answer is wrong, you could say, 'You were almost right. Let's try again together!'

- Show your child that calculations can be done using counters, on paper or in the head.

- Use everyday opportunities to practise multiplication and division. Try to find problems which are relevant to your child - for example, sharing out sweets, or working out how many cereal packets will be needed to collect enough tokens for the toy.

- Don't treat the tests too seriously. You can keep a running total of results on the chart on page 23. Encourage your child to sign the certificate when the book is completed. A sense of achievement is a great motivator!

Hodder Children's Books

The only home learning programme supported by the NCPTA

Counting in sets

When numbers are large, it is sometimes easier to count in equal groups, or **sets**.

1 bike has 1 set of 2 wheels.

2 bikes have 2 sets of 2 wheels, which is 4 wheels altogether.

3 bikes have 3 sets of 2 wheels, which is 6 wheels altogether.

Each of these children has two feet. We can say that each child has a set of feet.

1 child has [1] set of feet = [2] feet altogether

2 children have [ ] sets of feet = [ ] feet altogether

3 children have [ ] sets of feet = [ ] feet altogether

4 children have [ ] sets of feet = [ ] feet altogether

5 children have [ ] sets of feet = [ ] feet altogether

1 car has	4	wheels	6 cars have		wheels
2 cars have		wheels	7 cars have		wheels
3 cars have		wheels	8 cars have		wheels
4 cars have		wheels	9 cars have		wheels
5 cars have		wheels	10 cars have		wheels

Now try drawing these equal sets yourself.

Draw 3 cakes on each plate.   2 sets of 3 =

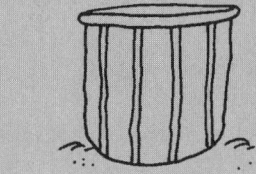

Draw 3 pencils in each pot.   3 sets of 3 =

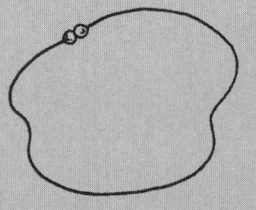

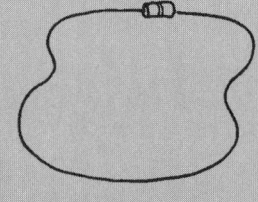

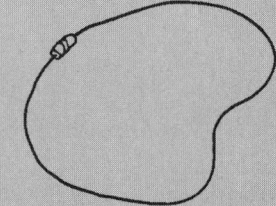

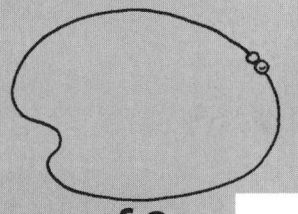

Draw 3 beads on each string.   4 sets of 3 =

More counting in equal sets

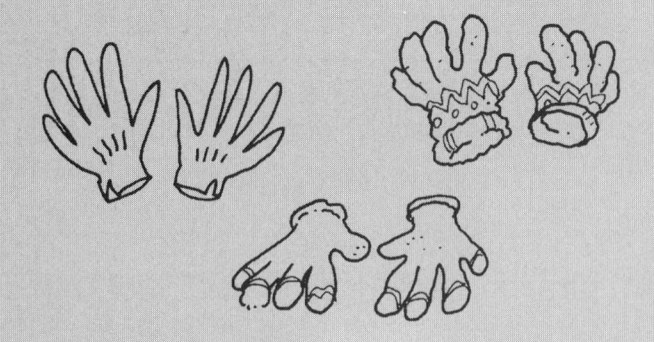

3 sets of 2 = 6

3 sets of 5 =

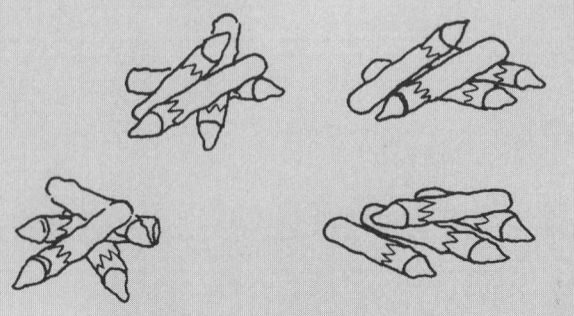

2 sets of ☐ = 12

☐ sets of 4 = 16

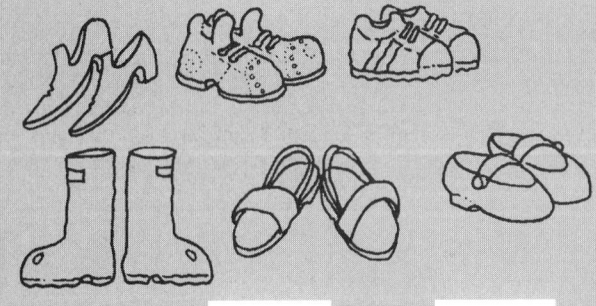

6 sets of ☐ = ☐

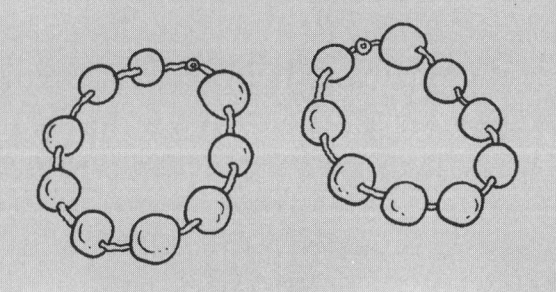

☐ sets of 9 = ☐

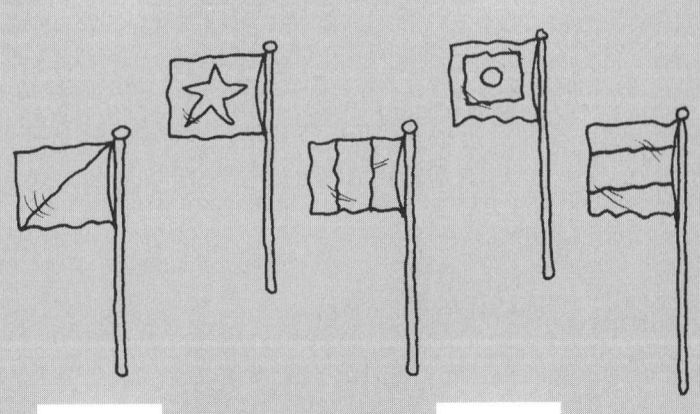

☐ sets of ☐ = 12

☐ sets of 1 =

4

Using the multiplication sign

**Instead of writing sets of, we can use the sign x.
This means multiplied by, or times.**

2 sets of 3 = 6
can be written as
2 x 3 = 6

This is the same as
3 + 3 = 6

3 sets of 3 = 9
can be written as
3 x ☐ = 9

This is the same as
3 + 3 + 3 = 9

2 sets of 4 = 8
can be written as
2 x ☐ = 8

This is the same as
4 + 4 = 8

3 sets of 0 = 0
can be written as
3 x ☐ = 0

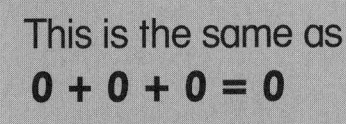

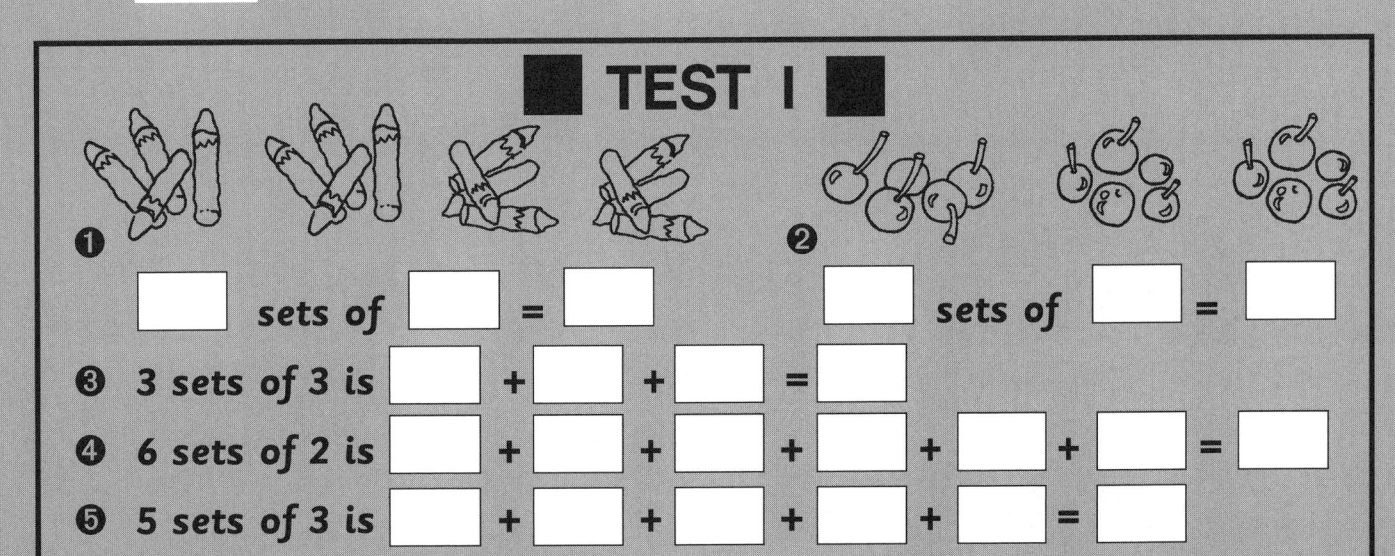

This is the same as
0 + 0 + 0 = 0

TEST 1

❶ ☐ sets of ☐ = ☐

❷ ☐ sets of ☐ = ☐

❸ 3 sets of 3 is ☐ + ☐ + ☐ = ☐

❹ 6 sets of 2 is ☐ + ☐ + ☐ + ☐ + ☐ + ☐ = ☐

❺ 5 sets of 3 is ☐ + ☐ + ☐ + ☐ + ☐ = ☐

This is the same as 5 x ☐ = ☐

SCORE ☐ / 5

Number sentences

can be written as

3 + 3 ⟶ 2 sets of 3 = ☐

5 + 5 ⟶ 2 sets of 5 = ☐

4 + 4 + 4 ⟶ 3 sets of 4 = ☐

6 + 6 ⟶ 2 x 6 = ☐

3 + 3 + 3 ⟶ 3 x 3 = ☐

6 + 6 + 6 ⟶ 3 x 6 = ☐

2 + 2 + 2 + 2 ⟶ 4 x 2 = ☐

3 + 3 + 3 + 3 + 3 ⟶ 5 x 3 = ☐

0 + 7 ⟶ 0 x 7 = ☐ (Think carefully about this one!)

Now try these. You may like to draw the sets to help you.

3 x 5 = ☐   4 x 6 = ☐

2 x 5 = ☐   7 x 3 = ☐

2 x 7 = ☐   3 x 6 = ☐

Problems!

1 Each vase has 5 flowers.
How many flowers are there altogether?   2 x ☐ = ☐

2 Each plate has 3 cakes on it.
How many cakes are there altogether?   4 x ☐ = ☐

3 Each basket holds 2 chicks.
How many chicks are there altogether?   ☐ x ☐ = ☐

4 Each house has 3 windows.
How many windows are there altogether?   ☐ x ☐ = ☐

TEST 2

❶ 3 x 6 = ☐
❷ 5 + 5 + 5 = ☐ x ☐ = 15
❸ 5 x 3 = ☐
❹ 2 x 4 = ☐
❺ 6 x 3 = ☐

❻ 2 x 9 = ☐
❼ 2 x 8 = ☐
❽ 2 x 7 = ☐
❾ 2 x 6 = ☐
❿ 2 x 5 = ☐

SCORE ☐/10

Multiplication

Counting equal sets is what we call multiplying numbers, or **multiplication**. Multiplication sums can be written in more than one way.

For example

6	sets of 2	=	12
6	multiplied by 2	equals	12
6	x 2	=	12
6	times 2	=	12

Counting in equal sets of 2 or 3 or 4 and so on gives special number patterns. These are called the multiplication tables, or times tables. Here are the 2 times, 5 times and 10 times tables.

2x

0 x 2 = 0
1 x 2 = 2
2 x 2 = 4
3 x 2 = 6
4 x 2 = 8
5 x 2 = 10
6 x 2 = 12
7 x 2 = 14
8 x 2 = 16
9 x 2 = 18
10 x 2 = 20
11 x 2 = 22
12 x 2 = 24

5x

0 x 5 = 0
1 x 5 = 5
2 x 5 = 10
3 x 5 = 15
4 x 5 = 20
5 x 5 = 25
6 x 5 = 30
7 x 5 = 35
8 x 5 = 40
9 x 5 = 45
10 x 5 = 50
11 x 5 = 55
12 x 5 = 60

10x

0 x 10 = 0
1 x 10 = 10
2 x 10 = 20
3 x 10 = 30
4 x 10 = 40
5 x 10 = 50
6 x 10 = 60
7 x 10 = 70
8 x 10 = 80
9 x 10 = 90
10 x 10 = 100
11 x 10 = 110
12 x 10 = 120

Try using these tables to match the numbers up, so the multiplication sums are correct.

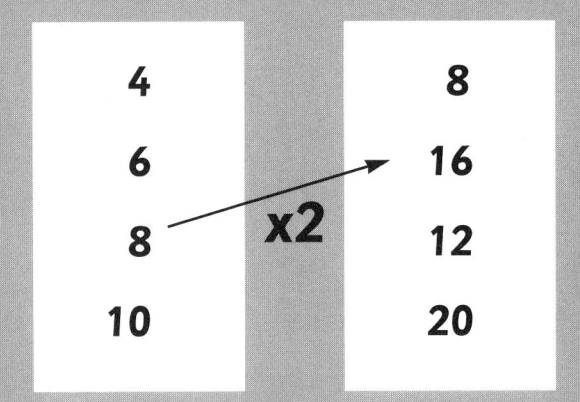

4	8
6	16
8	12
10	20

x2

0	20
3	15
4	0
2	10

x5

10	20
2	40
4	100
3	30

x10

Back to front tables

3 times 5 equals 15.

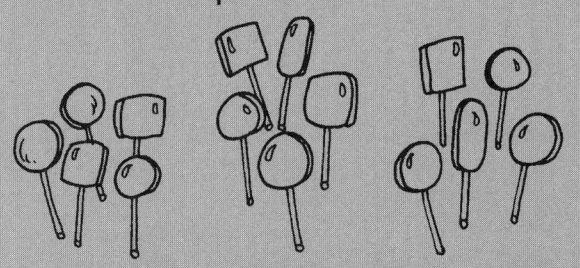

But 5 times 3 also equals 15.

3 x 5 = 15

5 x 3 = 15

Now try these and see what happens.

3 x 6 =

6 x 3 =

6 x 4 =

4 x 6 =

3 x 4 =

4 x 3 =

Using the times tables

Here are the 3 and 4 times tables.

0	x	3	=	0		0	x	4	=	0
1	x	3	=	3		1	x	4	=	4
2	x	3	=	6		2	x	4	=	8
3	x	3	=	9		3	x	4	=	12
4	x	3	=	12		4	x	4	=	16
5	x	3	=	15		5	x	4	=	20
6	x	3	=	18		6	x	4	=	24
7	x	3	=	21		7	x	4	=	28
8	x	3	=	24		8	x	4	=	32
9	x	3	=	27		9	x	4	=	36
10	x	3	=	30		10	x	4	=	40
11	x	3	=	33		11	x	4	=	44
12	x	3	=	36		12	x	4	=	48

Use the tables to help you work out these.

☐ x 5 = 15

3 x ☐ = 9

☐ x 4 = 16

8 x ☐ = 24

☐ x 4 = 40

☐ x 3 = 36

☐ x 4 = 0

6 x ☐ = 24

A tables square

0	1	2	3	4	5
1	1	2	3	4	5
2	2	4	6	8	10
3	3	6	9	12	15
4	4	8	12	16	20
5	5	10	15	20	25

This square does multiplication for you! For example, to work out 3 x 4, first find 3 along the top edge of the square. Then find 4 down the left edge of the square. Run your fingers along each row until they meet. Your total should be 12.

Now try using the tables square to do these multiplication sums.

2 x 4 = ☐   5 x 5 = ☐   3 x 3 = ☐

Multiplication and money

Prices: crisps 10p, biscuits 7p, apples 4p, pears 4p, raisins 8p

Can you work out how much these things cost?

1. 2 pears cost   2 x ☐ = ☐ pence
2. 2 packets of crisps cost   2 x ☐ = ☐ pence
3. 3 apples cost   ☐ x ☐ = ☐ pence
4. 5 packets of biscuits cost ☐ x ☐ = ☐ pence
5. 3 jars of raisins cost   ☐ x ☐ = ☐ pence

TEST 3

1. 5 jars of raisins cost ☐ pence

2.
```
   5        10
 x 10      x 5
 ____      ____
  ☐         ☐
```

3. ☐ x 4 = 48
4. ☐ x 10 = 20
5. 10 x 5 = ☐

6. ☐ x 9 = 45

7.
```
   5        9
 x 9      x 5
 ___      ___
  ☐        ☐
```

8. 3 packets of biscuits cost ☐ pence
9. ☐ x 11 = 22
10. 2 x ☐ = 22

SCORE ☐ / 10

Division

If we share a number into equal groups, it is called **division**.
For example, if we share 8 into two equal groups, there are 4 in each group.

We can also find out how many equal groups there are in a number.
For example, how many groups of 2 are there in 12?
There are 6 groups of 2 in 12.

Now try sharing 10 into two equal groups.

There are ☐ in each group.

Try sharing 12 into three equal groups.

There are ☐ in each group.

Can you share 15 into 5 equal groups?

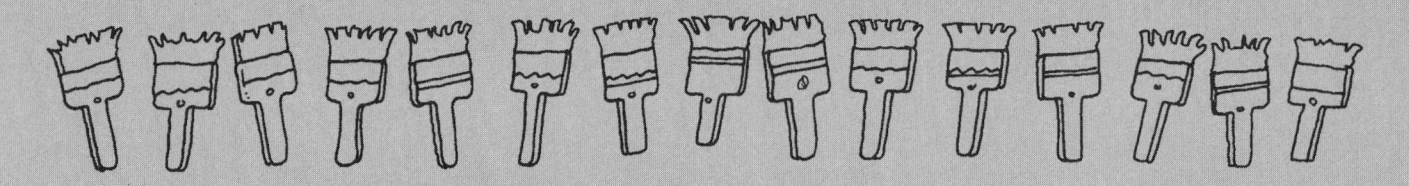

There are ☐ in each group.

How many equal groups of 3 are there in 9?

There are ☐ equal groups of 3 in 9.

How many equal groups of 2 are there in 10?

There are ☐ equal groups of 2 in 10.

How many equal groups of 4 are there in 12?

There are ☐ equal groups of 4 in 12.

How many equal groups of 5 are there in 15?

There are ☐ equal groups of 5 in 15.

Using the division sign

This is the division sign. ÷
It means **divide by**, **share** or **make into equal groups**.
For example, 10 ÷ 2 = 5 means
10 divided by 2 = 5
10 shared by 2 = 5
and 10 made into 2 equal groups = 5.

We can also use the division sign like this
$$\frac{10}{2}$$
This also means 10 divided by 2.

Here are 10 balloons divided up into groups of 2. There are 5 groups.

We can say that 10, shared out into groups of 2, gives 5 groups.

We write 10 divided by 2 equals 5.

This is the same as **10 ÷ 2 = 5.**

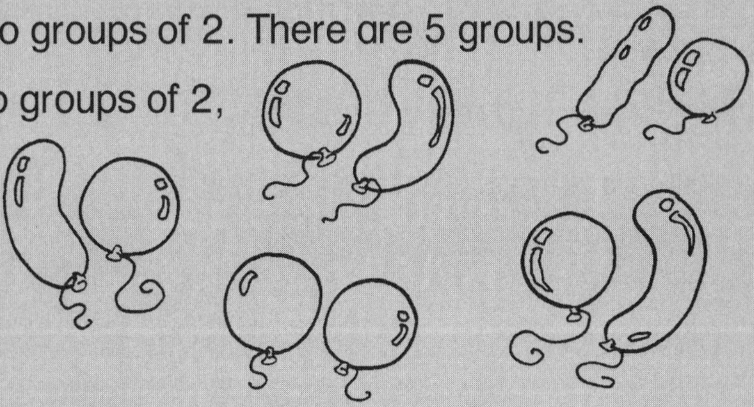

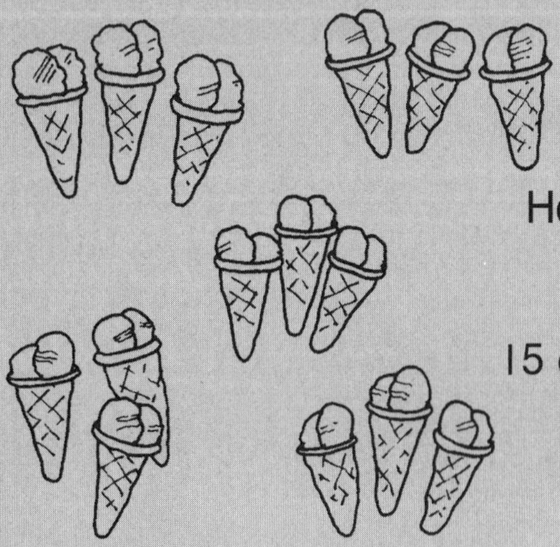

How many ice creams are there altogether? ☐

How many groups of 3? ☐

15 divided up into groups of 3 gives ☐ groups.

15 divided by 3 equals ☐

15 ÷ 3 = ☐

How many groups of 4? ☐

☐ divided by ☐ equals ☐

☐ ÷ ☐ = ☐

Problems!

John, Peter, Sam and Ranjit share 16 sweets equally. How many sweets does each boy get?

$\frac{16}{4}$ = 16 ÷ 4 = ☐

How many 2s are there in 18?

$\frac{18}{2}$ = 18 ÷ 2 = ☐

TEST 4

1. How many 3s make 12?

   $\frac{12}{3}$ = ☐

2. Share 15 cakes between 5 people.

   15 ÷ 5 = ☐

3. Share 12 into 6 equal groups

   There are ☐ in each group.

4. How many equal groups of 3 are there in 9?

   9 ÷ 3 = ☐

5. $\frac{10}{5}$ = ☐

6. $\frac{12}{2}$ = ☐

7. $\frac{14}{7}$ = ☐

8. $\frac{8}{4}$ = ☐

9. 6 ÷ 3 = ☐

10. 10 ÷ 2 = ☐

11. 12 ÷ 3 = ☐

12. 16 ÷ 8 = ☐

13. Share 12 toys among 6 children.
    Each child gets ☐ toys.

14. Divide 10 by 2 ☐

15. How many groups of 2 in 12? ☐

SCORE / 15

Using the number line

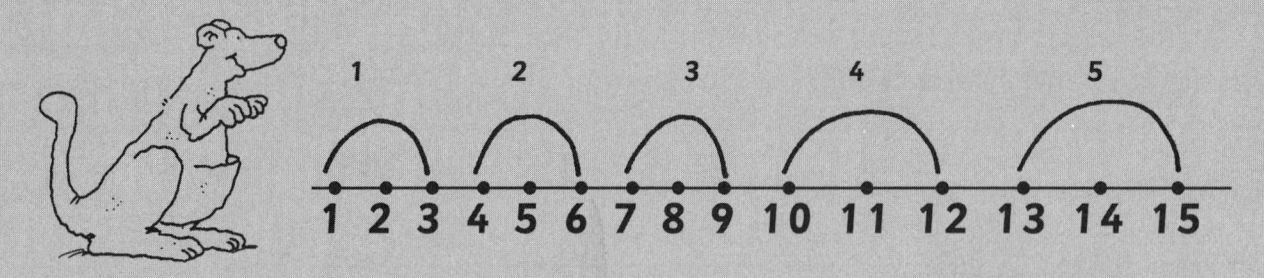

Using a number line can make division easier. This number line shows 15 grouped into 3s, or 15 divided by 3. It's easy to see that there are 5 groups.

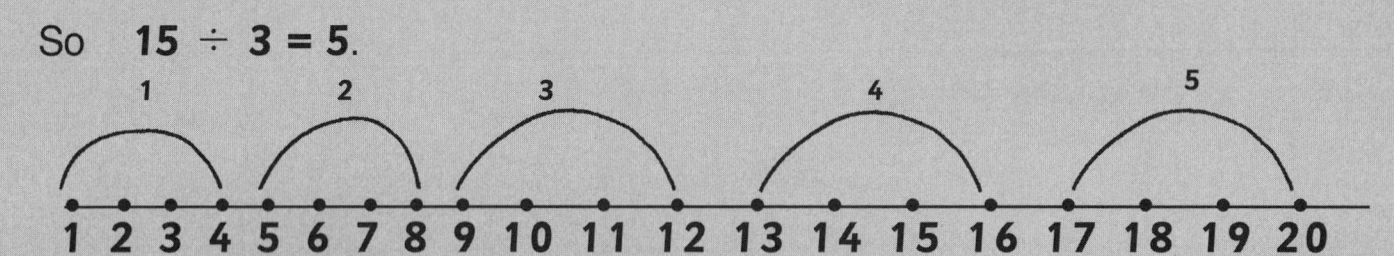

So 15 ÷ 3 = 5.

This number line shows 20 grouped into 4s.

20 grouped into 4s gives ☐ groups.   20 ÷ 4 = ☐

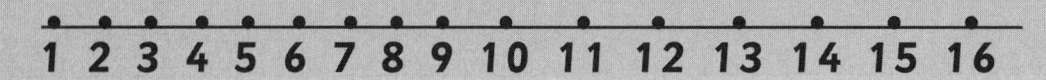

Try grouping this number line of 16 into 2s.

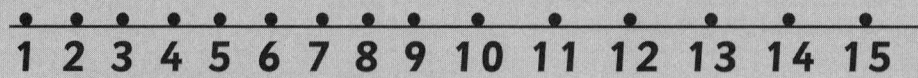

16 ÷ 2 = ☐

Group this number line of 15 into 5s.

15 ÷ 5 = ☐

Show this number line of 18 grouped into 2s.

18 ÷ 2 = ☐

Back to front division

Division undoes what is done by multiplication.

So   **2 x 4 = 8**   can be written as   **8 ÷ 2 = 4**

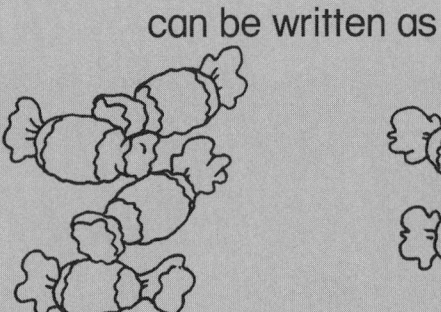

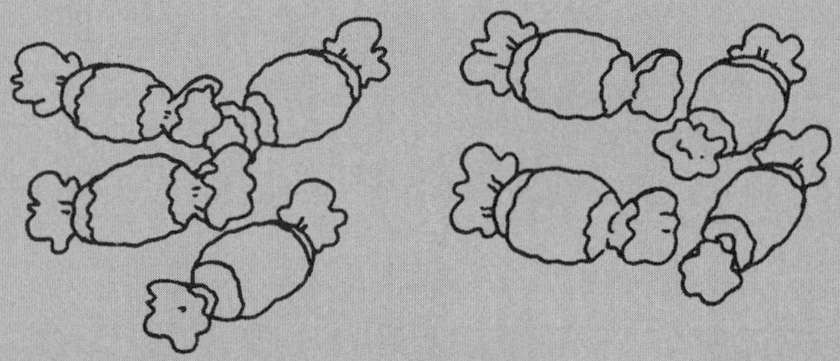

Have a go at these.

4 x ▢ = 12   can be written as   12 ÷ 4 = ▢

5 x ▢ = 15   can be written as   15 ÷ 5 = ▢

3 x ▢ = 9   can be written as   9 ÷ 3 = ▢

2 x ▢ = 14   can be written as   14 ÷ 2 = ▢

x	1	2	3	4	5	6	7
1	1	2	3	4	5	6	7
2	2	4	6	8	10	12	14
3	3	6	9	12	15	18	21
4	4	8	12	16	20	24	28
5	5	10	15	20	25	30	35
6	6	12	18	24	30	36	42
7	7	14	21	28	35	42	49

We can use the tables square for working out division sums.

To work out **12 ÷ 4**, look down the column on the left of the square to find 4. Then go across this row until you find 12. Finally, go directly up this row to the top of the square. The number at the top of the column should be 3.

So   **12 ÷ 4 = 3**

Try using the square to find the answers for these:

20 ÷ 5 = ▢   42 ÷ 7 = ▢   16 ÷ 4 = ▢

18 ÷ 3 = ▢   12 ÷ 3 = ▢   36 ÷ 6 = ▢

Division sums can be set out in two ways.

10 ÷ 2 = 5   or   2)10̄ = 5

10 divided by 2 equals 5   2 goes into 10, 5 times

Try these. The tables square on page 17 might help you.

6)12   12 ÷ 6 = ☐   7)14   14 ÷ 7 = ☐

5)20   20 ÷ 5 = ☐   8)24   24 ÷ 8 = ☐

Remainders

When we're dividing into equal groups, we are sometimes left with too few to make another equal group. The amount left over is called the remainder.

3)14

We can make 4 groups of 3 but there are 2 left over. We write   3)14 = 4 r 2

Now try these.

5)16

2)13

7)16

TEST 5

1 0 1 2 3 4 5 6 7 8 9 10 11 12 13 14

Show 14 in groups of 2.   14 ÷ 2 = ☐

2 17 children stand in groups of 3. How many are left over? ☐

3 5 x ☐ = 10 can be written as 10 ÷ 5 = ☐

4 ☐ x 6 = 12 can be written as 12 ÷ ☐ = 6

5 Share 8 sweets equally among 3 girls.
How many sweets does each girl get? ☐
How many sweets are left over? ☐

Use the tables square for these:

6 28 ÷ 7 = ☐   **7** 20 ÷ 4 = ☐   **8** 24 ÷ 8 = ☐

9 21 ÷ 3 = ☐   **10** 10 ÷ 2 = ☐

11 5)10   **12** 4)16   **13** 3)12

14 2)14   **15** 6)18

16 2)10   **17** 5)15

Don't forget the remainders in these:

18 3)16   **19** 5)13   **20** 2)11

SCORE /20

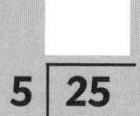

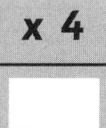

Multiply or divide

3 x 2 = ☐   2 x 3 = ☐   10 ÷ 2 = ☐

15 ÷ 3 = ☐   5 x 4 = ☐   4 x 5 = ☐

9 ÷ 3 = ☐   8 ÷ 4 = ☐

```
  TU          TU          TU          TU          TU
   2           2           4           3           3
  x 3         x 4         x 5         x 6         x 4
  ───         ───         ───         ───         ───
```

3)9   2)8   5)10   3)6   4)8

Use the tables square to do these.

```
  TU                      TU
   5          7)21         6          5)25
  x 4                     x 3
  ───                     ───
```

```
  TU                      TU
   7          9)18         5          8)16
  x 2                     x 4
  ───                     ───
```

Missing numbers

3 x ☐ = 15   7 x ☐ = 14
6 x ☐ = 18   ☐ x 5 = 20
☐ x 6 = 18   4 x ☐ = 16

TU   TU   TU   TU
☐   4   6   ☐
x 3   x ☐   x ☐   x 2
―――   ―――   ―――   ―――
 9   8   24   10

12 ÷ ☐ = 6   14 ÷ ☐ = 7   15 ÷ ☐ = 3
10 ÷ ☐ = 5   12 ÷ ☐ = 4   20 ÷ ☐ = 10

Problems

5 children each have 4 books. How many books are there altogether?

☐

3 apples cost 21 pence. How much does one apple cost?

☐

Cakes are in packets of 3. How many cakes are there in 8 packets?

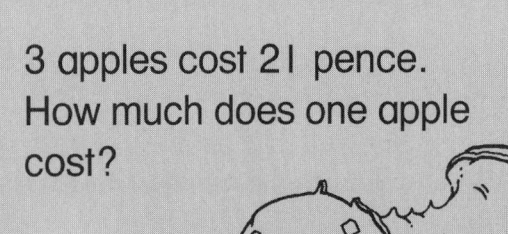

☐

Share 12 sweets between 3 children. How many sweets does each child get?

☐

TEST 6

❶ 6 x 3 = ☐   ❷ 8 x 2 = ☐   ❸ 4 x 5 = ☐

❹ 9 ÷ 3 = ☐   ❺ 14 ÷ 2 = ☐   ❻ 18 ÷ 3 = ☐

❼ TU
   4
x 5
———
☐

❽ TU
   2
x 9
———
☐

❾ TU
   4
x 4
———
☐

❿ TU
   8
x 2
———
☐

⑪ 7) 14   ☐
⑫ 8) 16   ☐
⑬ 5) 20   ☐
⑭ 3) 18   ☐

⑮ 2 x ☐ = 10   can be written as   10 ÷ 2 = ☐

⑯ 3 x ☐ = 18   can be written as   18 ÷ 3 = ☐

⑰ TU
☐
x 3
———
18

⑱ TU
4
x ☐
———
8

⑲ TU
☐
x 4
———
12

⑳ TU
☐
x 6
———
18

㉑ 14 ÷ ☐ = 2   ㉒ 15 ÷ ☐ = 3   ㉓ 18 ÷ ☐ = 9

㉔ There are 5 chairs in a row.
How many chairs are there in 4 rows? ☐

㉕ If we have 24 eggs, how many boxes of six can we fill? ☐

SCORE / 25

RECORD OF SUCCESS

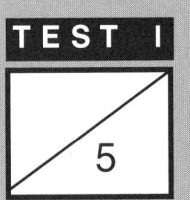

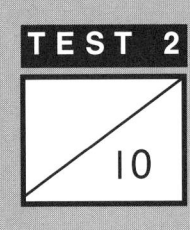

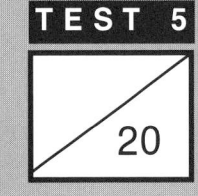

TEST 1	TEST 2	TEST 3	TEST 4	TEST 5	TEST 6
5	10	10	15	20	25

TOTAL: 85

******* CERTIFICATE *******

This is to certify that

_____

has successfully finished this book and has done very well.

signed _____

date _____

Answers

Test 1
1. 4 sets of 4 = 16
2. 3 sets of 5 = 15
3. 3 + 3 + 3 = 9
4. 2 + 2 + 2 + 2 + 2 + 2 = 12
5. 3 + 3 + 3 + 3 + 3 = 15
   5 × 3 = 15

Test 2
1. 3 × 6 = 18
2. 3 × 5 = 15
3. 5 × 3 = 15
4. 2 × 4 = 8
5. 6 × 3 = 18
6. 2 × 9 = 18
7. 2 × 8 = 16
8. 2 × 7 = 14
9. 2 × 6 = 12
10. 2 × 5 = 10

Test 3
1. 5 × 8p = 40p
2. 5 × 10 = 50, 10 × 5 = 50
3. 12 × 4 = 48
4. 2 × 10 = 20
5. 10 × 5 = 50
6. 5 × 9 = 45
7. 5 × 9 = 45, 9 × 5 = 45
8. 3 × 7 = 21p
9. 2 × 11 = 22
10. 2 × 11 = 22

Test 4
1. $\frac{12}{3} = 4$
2. 15 ÷ 5 = 3
3. 12 ÷ 6 = 2
4. 9 ÷ 3 = 3
5. $\frac{10}{5} = 2$
6. $\frac{12}{2} = 6$
7. $\frac{14}{7} = 2$
8. $\frac{8}{4} = 2$
9. 6 ÷ 3 = 2
10. 10 ÷ 2 = 5
11. 12 ÷ 3 = 4
12. 16 ÷ 8 = 2
13. 12 ÷ 6 = 2
14. 10 ÷ 2 = 5
15. 12 ÷ 2 = 6

Test 5
1. 14 ÷ 2 = 7
2. 17 ÷ 3 = 5 r2
3. 5 × 2 = 10 can be written as 10 ÷ 5 = 2
4. 2 × 6 = 12 can be written as 12 ÷ 2 = 6
5. Each girl gets 2 sweets. There are 2 sweets left over.
6. 28 ÷ 7 = 4
7. 20 ÷ 4 = 5
8. 24 ÷ 8 = 3
9. 21 ÷ 3 = 7
10. 10 ÷ 2 = 5
11. 10 ÷ 5 = 2
12. 16 ÷ 4 = 4
13. 12 ÷ 3 = 4
14. 14 ÷ 2 = 7
15. 18 ÷ 6 = 3
16. 10 ÷ 2 = 5
17. 15 ÷ 5 = 3
18. 16 ÷ 3 = 5 r1
19. 13 ÷ 5 = 2 r3
20. 11 ÷ 2 = 5 r1

Test 6
1. 6 × 3 = 18
2. 8 × 2 = 16
3. 4 × 5 = 20
4. 9 ÷ 3 = 3
5. 14 ÷ 2 = 7
6. 18 ÷ 3 = 6
7. 4 × 5 = 20
8. 2 × 9 = 18
9. 4 × 4 = 16
10. 8 × 2 = 16
11. 14 ÷ 7 = 2
12. 16 ÷ 8 = 2
13. 20 ÷ 5 = 4
14. 18 ÷ 3 = 6
15. 2 × 5 = 10 can be written as 10 ÷ 2 = 5
16. 3 × 6 = 18 can be written as 18 ÷ 3 = 6
17. 6 × 3 = 18
18. 4 × 2 = 8
19. 3 × 4 = 12
20. 3 × 6 = 18
21. 14 ÷ 7 = 2
22. 15 ÷ 5 = 3
23. 18 ÷ 2 = 9
24. There are 20 chairs altogether.
25. We can fill 4 boxes.

ISBN 0 340 62984 3
Copyright © 1995 Rhona Whiteford and Jim Fitzsimmons

The rights of Rhona Whiteford and Jim Fitzsimmons to be identified as the authors of this work has been asserted by them in accordance with the Copyright, Design and Patent Act 1988.

First published in Great Britain 1995

10 9 8 7 6 5 4 3 2 1

All rights reserved. No part of this publication may be reproduced, stored in a retrieval system, or transmitted, in any form or by any means, without the prior written permission of the publisher, nor be otherwise circulated in any form of binding or cover other than that in which it is published and without a similar condition being imposed on the subsequent purchaser.

Published by Hodder Children's Books, a division of Hodder Headline plc, 338 Euston Road, London NW1 3BH.
Printed in Great Britain.
A CIP record is registered by and held at the British Library.